Past Papers
Question Bank AMC 10

vol. II

Comprehensive Collection of AMC10 Past Papers

AMC10 Past Paper Questions Categorized by Topic

Introduction

Welcome to the world of AMC10 problem-solving! In this book by Kay, we present a unique approach to help students excel in the AMC10 examination. The book's distinct features aim to enhance performance and guide students towards better results.

The first notable aspect is the organization. Problems from past AMC10 exams are categorized by content, allowing students to focus on specific topics and develop a deeper understanding. By providing a structured learning experience, students can strengthen their problem-solving skills.

Another crucial element is the careful determination of problem difficulty. Each problem is ranked according to its level of complexity, ensuring a diverse range of challenges. Similar problems closely aligned with the actual exam questions provide additional practice opportunities, familiarizing students with the exam format.

Comprehensive learning is ensured through detailed solutions. Step-by-step explanations accompany each problem, guiding students through the thought processes and strategies for arriving at correct answers. This empowers students to approach problems confidently and strengthen their abilities.

The book's purpose is to equip students with the necessary tools to achieve better results in the AMC10 examination. By providing curated problems, determining difficulty levels, and offering in-depth solutions, we aim to enhance performance and foster a passion for mathematics.

Embark on this journey of problem-solving, and let the challenges within these pages propel you towards success in the AMC10 examination!

Table of Contents

53.

As shown, the rectangle is divided into five sections. Using red, black, yellow, brown, and green, paint each of the five sections a single color while ensuring that no touching regions have the same color and that colors can be repeated.

What is the total number of possible color arrangements?

(AMC 10A, 12A problem)

(A)　60

(B)　120

(C)　240

(D)　420

(E)　540

Solving Strategy

Use the counting principle and work through the partitions one by one, starting with the top left rectangle.

54. ▐▐▐▐▐▐▐▐☐

The traditional Korean kite shown in the image displays a circular Taegeuk design on its upper portion, which contrasts with the white background. The lower part of the kite is separated into seven rectangular parts, each of which is painted in a different color than the

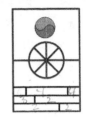

adjacent sections. Each section is to be painted a solid color - red, yellow, blue, or green - so that sections that touch are painted different colors, and colors can be used more than once.

How many different colorings are possible?

(AMC 10A, 12A similar problem)

(A)   64

(B)   120

(C)   288

(D)   320

(E)   0 (impossible)

55. ■■■■□

Examine sets of three linear equations in the form;

$$p_1x + q_1y + r_1z = 0$$
$$p_2x + q_2y + r_2z = 0$$
$$p_3x + q_3y + r_3z = 0$$

where every coefficient is either 0 or 1, and the system has a non-zero solution. An instance of such a system with a nonzero solution is

$$1x + 1y + 0z = 0, \quad 0x + 1y + 1z = 0, \quad 0x + 0y + 0z = 0,$$

and the solution is $(x, y, z) = (1, -2, -1)$.

What is the total number of systems of equations that satisfy the given criteria?
(Two systems of equations that contain the same equations, even if they are arranged differently, are regarded as distinct, and the equations within a single system need not be unique.)

(AMC 10B problem)

(A)   332

(B)   334

(C)   336

(D)   338

(E)   340

◽ **Solving Strategy**

We will use complementary counting and do casework on the equations. We will consider the eight possible equations and then divide the problem into cases based on which equations are present in the system.

How many four-digit positive integers have at least one digit that is a 1 or a 5?

(AMC 10B similar problem)

(A)   5,412

(B)   5,414

(C)   5,416

(D)   5,418

(E)   5,420

57. ■■□□□

What is the count of three-digit positive integers with an odd number of even digits?

(AMC 10B problem)

(A)   350

(B)   400

(C)   450

(D)   500

(E)   550

Solving Strategy

The problem can be solved using the complement principle by finding the number of three-digit positive integers with an even number of even digits and subtracting that from the total number of three-digit positive integers.

58. ⬛⬛⬜⬜⬜

A box contains 17 red socks, 16 green socks, 12 yellow socks, 10 blue socks, 8 white socks, and 6 black socks.

What is the minimum number of balls that must be drawn from the box without replacement to guarantee that at least 11 socks of a single color will be drawn?

(AMC 10B similar problem)

(A)   51

(B)   52

(C)   53

(D)   54

(E)   55

59. ■■■■□

What is the number of ways to divide the integers 1 through 14 into 7 pairs such that in each pair, the greater number is at least 2 times the lesser number?

(AMC 10A, 12A problem)

(A) $2 \times 7!$

(B) $14!$

(C) $7!$

(D) $6 \times 4!$

(E) $4 \times 6!$

We can use casework to solve this problem. First, we can identify the pairs that must be formed based on the condition that the greater number is at least 2 times the lesser number. Then, we can use casework to determine the number of ways to form the remaining pairs.

60. ▮▮▮▮▯

Duke has colored paper squares with side lengths ranging from 1 to 16 integers. How many possible ways are there to divide all of these squares into 8 pairs, where each pair satisfies the condition that the length of the larger side is at least twice the length of the smaller side?

(AMC 10A, 12A similar problem)

(A)   428

(B)   576

(C)   612

(D)   784

(E)   840

61. ▮▮▮▮▮▮

Suppose we have a deck of 52 standard cards, including cards numbered 1 through 10 as well as Jack, Queen, and King. If we arrange these 13 cards in a row, we can assign the values 1 through 13 to them, with Jack being 11, Queen being 12, and King being 13. The objective is to select the cards in ascending numerical order, continuously moving from the leftmost position to the right.

For how many of the 13! possible orderings of the cards will the 13 cards be picked up in exactly two passes?

(AMC 10A, 12A problem)

(A)   7700

(B)   7814

(C)   7936

(D)   8052

(E)   8178

🔲 Solving Strategy

To solve this problem, we can first assume that 1, 2, ..., k cards are picked up in the first pass and then find the number of ways to arrange the remaining cards in the second pass. Then, we can sum over all possible values of k and add 1 to exclude the arrangement in which all 13 cards are picked up in the first pass.

62. ■■■□□

Assume that a sequence of cards consisting of the numbers 1 through 10 is placed in a horizontal line. The task is to pick them up in numerically increasing order, working repeatedly from left to right.

For how many of the 10! possible orderings of the cards will the 10 cards be picked up in exactly two passes?

(AMC 10A, 12A similar problem)

(A)   971

(B)   989

(C)   997

(D)   1013

(E)   1125

63. ■■■■■

What is the count of 5-digit strings created using the digits $0, 1, 2, 3, 4$, where for each value $n = \{1, 2, 3, 4\}$, there are at least n digits in the string that are strictly less than n?
(For example, 01234 satisfies this condition because it contains at least 1 digit less than 1, at least 2 digits less than 2, at least 3 digits less than 3, and at least 4 digits less than 4. The string 24313 does not satisfy the condition because it does not contain at least 2 digits less than 2.)

(AMC 10A, 12A problem)

(A)   1010

(B)   1154

(C)   1296

(D)   1372

(E)   1438

Solving Strategy

To solve this problem, we need to use counting principles and casework. We should start by considering the rule given in the problem and use it to deduce what kind of strings are valid. Then we can perform casework on the number of different digits such strings can have, list the digits in ascending order, and consider permutations.

64. ▮▮▮▮☐

Consider the set N of permutations of the sequence $1, 2, 3, 4, 5$ such that the first term is not 1. Suppose that a permutation is selected at random from the set N. Expressed in lowest terms, the probability that the second term is 2 is equal to $\frac{x}{y}$.

What is the sum of x and y?

(AMC 10A, 12A similar problem)

(A)   17

(B)   18

(C)   19

(D)   20

(E)   21

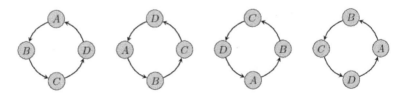

65. ▮▮▮▮▯

Beginning at 0 on the number line, flea Frederick proceeds to jump as follows. Flea Frederick selects random values of time duration t_n and increment x_n from the interval $(0, 1)$ independently and uniformly at each jump, where $n = 1, 2, 3, \ldots$. Frederick jumps x_n units to the right and spends t_n minutes during the nth jump of the process. If the sum of the time elapsed during the n jumps is greater than 1 minute, Frederick stops at the end of the n th jump; otherwise, he continues with the next jump, taking at most 3 jumps in total.

What is the probability that Frederick's position when he stops will be greater than 1?

(AMC 10B, 12B problem)

(A) $\dfrac{1}{2}$

(B) $\dfrac{2}{3}$

(C) $\dfrac{1}{4}$

(D) $\dfrac{3}{4}$

(E) $\dfrac{3}{5}$

Solving Strategy

We can solve this problem by breaking it down into two cases: Frederick takes exactly 2 steps, or Frederick takes exactly 3 steps. For each case, we need to determine the probability that his position when he stops is greater than 1.

66. ▮▮▮▮▯

Assume that R is a square with sides of length 1. Two points are chosen independently at random on the sides of R. Let x, y, and z be positive integers coprime (no common factor other than 1) to each other. Then the probability that the straight-line distance between two points selected uniformly at random from the sides of R is greater than or equal to $\frac{1}{2}$ can be expressed as $\frac{x+y\pi}{z}$.

What is the sum of x, y, and z?

(AMC 10B, 12B similar problem)

(A) 55

(B) 56

(C) 57

(D) 58

(E) 59

67. ■■■□□

A pair of fair 6-sided dice is rolled n times.

What is the least value of n such that the probability that the sum of the numbers face up on a roll equals 5 at least once is greater than $\frac{1}{2}$?

(AMC 10B problem)

(A)   4

(B)   5

(C)   6

(D)   7

(E)   8

Solving Strategy

First, find the probability of getting a sum of 5 on one roll of two dice. Then, use the complement rule to find the probability of not getting a sum of 5. Next, use the formula for the probability of an event occurring at least once in n trials, which is 1 minus the probability of the event not occurring in n trials. Set this expression greater than 1/3 and solve for the least value of n.

68. ⬛⬛☐☐☐

You roll four six-sided dice that are fair.

What is the probability that at least three of the four dice show the same value?

(AMC similar problem)

(A) $\dfrac{3}{38}$

(B) $\dfrac{4}{45}$

(C) $\dfrac{5}{54}$

(D) $\dfrac{6}{65}$

(E) $\dfrac{7}{72}$

69. ▦▦▦☐☐

The smallest positive integer that is divisible by both 18 and n is 180, and the largest positive integer that divides both n and 45 is 15.

What is a positive integer n?

(AMC 10A, 12A problem)

(A) 30

(B) 45

(C) 60

(D) 75

(E) 90

⌗ **Solving Strategy**

Smallest positive integer that is divisible by both 18 and n is LCM of 18 and n and largest positive integer that divides both n and 45 is GCF of n and 45.

The prime factorization of the given numbers can be used to find the prime factorization of n. The LCM and GCF conditions can be used to determine the values of $a, b,$ and c. Once we have the prime factorization of n, we can find the sum of its digits.

70. ■■□□□

The least common multiple of a positive integer m and 30 is 240, and the greatest common divisor of m and 60 is 20.

What is the sum of the digits of m?

(AMC 10A, 12A similar problem)

(A)   7

(B)   8

(C)   9

(D)   10

(E)   11

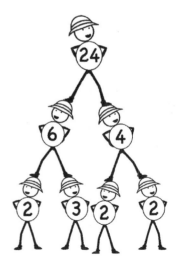

71. ◼◼◼◼◻

What is the number of distinct sets of three nonzero digits p, q, and r, such that the repeating decimal $0.\overline{pqr}$ is equal to one-third of the sum of the repeating decimals $0.\overline{p}$, $0.\overline{q}$, and $0.\overline{r}$?

(AMC 10A problem)

(A)   9

(B)   10

(C)   11

(D)   12

(E)   13

Solving Strategy

Recognize that the roots of the given polynomial correspond to the dimensions of a rectangular box. Use the formula for the volume of a rectangular box and substitute in the roots.
Find the new dimensions by adding 2 units to each dimension.
Use the same formula to find the volume of the new box.

72. ■■■□□

When a student multiplied the number 44 by the repeating decimal, $4.xyxy\ldots = 4.\overline{xy}$, where x and y are digits, she did not notice the notation and just multiplied 44 times $4.xy$. Later she found that her answer is 0.4 less than the correct answer.

What is the number represented by the digits xy?

(AMC 10A similar problem)

(A)   44

(B)   80

(C)   88

(D)   90

(E)   99

73. ▪▪▪☐☐

Two primes have a difference of 2, and the difference between the cubes of these two primes is 62,426.

What is the sum of the digits of the least prime that is greater than those two primes?

(AMC 10B problem)

(A) 8

(B) 12

(C) 16

(D) 22

(E) 24

⚙️ **Solving Strategy**

, Use the given information to form equations involving the two primes. Then, solve for the two primes and use them to find the next prime. Finally, find the sum of the digits of the next prime.

74. ▪▮☐☐☐

The smallest prime number that is a divisor of 17,408 is 2 because $17{,}408 = 17 \times 2^{10}$.

What is the sum of the digits of the greatest prime number that is a divisor of 17,391?

(AMC 10B similar problem)

(A) 4

(B) 5

(C) 6

(D) 7

(E) 8

75. ▆▆☐☐☐

Take into account these 100 sets, each comprising 10 elements:

$$\{1, 2, 3, ..., 10\},$$
$$\{11, 12, 13, ..., 20\},$$
$$...$$
$$\{991, 992, 993, ..., 1000\}.$$

How many of these sets contain exactly two multiples of 7?

(AMC 10B, 12B problem)

(A)   40

(B)   41   40 - 49

(C)   42

(D)   43

(E)   44

⌗ **Solving Strategy**

To solve this problem, we need to first identify the conditions under which a set of 10 elements contains exactly two multiples of 7. We can then use these conditions to count the number of sets that meet the criteria by applying casework.

76. ◼◼◼☐☐

Define $S(n)$ as the sum of digits of any positive integer n. For example, $S(2619) = 18$. If a particular positive integer n, $S(n) = 2065$.

What is a possible value for $S(n + 1)$ among the followings?

(AMC 10B, 12B similar problem)

(A)   1239

(B)   2954

(C)   3081

(D)   4326

(E)   5459

77. ◼◼☐☐☐

What is the numerical value of

$$3 + \cfrac{1}{3 + \cfrac{1}{3 + \cfrac{1}{3 + \frac{1}{3}}}} \ ?$$

(AMC 10A, 12A problem)

(A) $\dfrac{17}{66}$

(B) $\dfrac{16}{33}$

(C) $\dfrac{10}{33}$

(D) $\dfrac{14}{69}$

(E) $\dfrac{109}{33}$

$$\frac{33}{10}$$

$$\frac{10}{3} \qquad \frac{99}{100}$$

$$3 + \frac{100}{99}$$

$$\frac{297}{99} + \frac{100}{99}$$

$$\frac{397}{99}$$

⚙ *Solving Strategy*

The problem involves a nested fraction, which can be difficult to simplify directly. One approach is to work from the inside out, simplifying the nested fraction before adding it to 3. Another approach is to use algebraic manipulation to turn the entire expression into a single fraction that can be simplified.

78. ◼◼☐☐☐

What is the value of

$$5 + \cfrac{1}{5 + \cfrac{1}{5 + \cfrac{1}{5 + \frac{1}{5}}}} \ ?$$

AMC 10A, 12A similar problem)

(A) $\dfrac{67}{11}$

(B) $\dfrac{55}{213}$

(C) $\dfrac{213}{55}$

(D) $\dfrac{701}{135}$

(E) $\dfrac{135}{701}$

A cycle of 2 values

A cycle of 3 values

A cycle of 7 values

A cycle of 12 values

79. ■■■■□

Let S_n be the smallest positive integer that is divisible by all integers from 1 to n inclusive. The sum of the reciprocals of the integers from 1 to 17 inclusive can be expressed as;

$$\frac{1}{1}+\frac{1}{2}+\frac{1}{3}+ \ldots +\frac{1}{17} = \frac{k}{S_n}.$$

What is the remainder when k is divided by 17?

(AMC 10A problem)

(A)   4

(B)   5

(C)   14

(D)   15

(E)   16

Solving Strategy

This question involves finding the smallest positive integer that is divisible by all integers from 1 to n, and then using modular arithmetic to find the remainder when k is divided by 17. The strategy involves finding the least common multiple of all integers from 1 to 17 to get S_{17}, multiplying the denominators of the given expression by S_{17}, simplifying the expression using modular arithmetic, and then finding the remainder of the resulting expression when divided by 17.

Define C_n as the least common multiple of all the integers from 1 to n inclusive. There is a unique integer k such that

$$\frac{1}{2}+\frac{1}{3}+\frac{1}{4}+ \ldots +\frac{1}{12}+\frac{1}{13}=\frac{k}{C_{13}}.$$

What is the remainder when k is divided by 13?

(AMC 10A similar problem)

(A)   3

(B)   4

(C)   10

(D)   11

(E)   12

A cycle of 2 values

A cycle of 3 values

A cycle of 7 values

A cycle of 12 values

Consider squares A, B, and C in the coordinate plane whose vertices are located at lattice points (points with integer coordinates), and include their interiors. The x-axis intersects the bottom edge of each square.

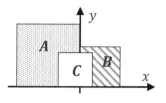

A has its left edge and B has its right edge on the y-axis, and the number of lattice points inside A is $\frac{9}{4}$ times that of B.

C shares its top two vertices with either A or B, and it contains one-fourth of the total number of lattice points in the union of A and B. Refer to the diagram (not to scale).

The ratio of lattice points contained in both A and B to the total number of lattice points in B is 27 times the ratio of lattice points contained in both A and C to the total number of lattice points in A.

What is the smallest possible sum of the edge lengths of A, B, and C?

(AMC 10A problem)

(A)   388

(B)   389

(C)   390

(D)   391

(E)   392

Solving Strategy

To solve this problem, use the fact that the number of lattice points in a square is equal to the number of lattice points along one side squared. Also, note that the length of a square can be represented by the number of lattice points along one side minus 1.

82. ▮▮▮▮▯

Let $n_1, n_2, \ldots, n_{2022}$ be an increasing sequence of positive integers such that $n_1 + n_2 + \ldots + n_{2022} = 2022^{2022}$.

What is the remainder when $n_1^3 + n_2^3 + \ldots + n_{2022}^3$ is divided by 6?

(AMC 10A similar problem)

(A)   0

(B)   1

(C)   2

(D)   3

(E)   4

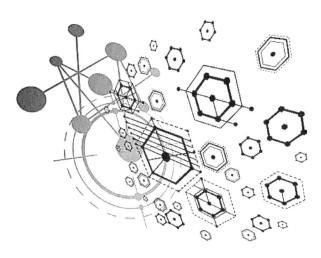

83.

Consider a sequence of numbers a_0, a_1, a_2, ... such that each element a_k is either 0 or 1. For each positive integer n, define;

$$S_n = \sum_{k=0}^{n-1} a_k \, 2^k$$

Given that $7S_n \equiv 1 \;(mod \; 2^n)$ for all $n \geq 1$, what is the value of the sum

$$a_{2019} + 2a_{2020} + 4a_{2021} + 8a_{2022}?$$

(AMC 10B, 12B problem)

(A)   5

(B)   6

(C)   128

(D)   136

(E)   142

Solving Strategy

Use the fact that $7S_n$ is congruent to 1 modulo 2^n to find S_{2019} and S_{2023}, and then use the given expression for $a_{2019} + 2a_{2020} + 4a_{2021} + 8a_{2022}$ in terms of S_n to calculate the final answer.

Let u_0, u_1, u_2, ... be a sequence of numbers, where each u_k is either 0 or 1.

For each positive integer n, define:

$$S_n = \sum_{k=0}^{n-1} x_k 2^k$$

Suppose $5S_n \equiv 2 \pmod{2^n}$ for all $n \geq 1$.

What is the value of the sum

$$u_{2020} + 2u_{2021} + 4u_{2022} + 8u_{2023}?$$

(AMC 10B, 12B similar problem)

(A) 4

(B) 5

(C) 6

(D) 7

(E) 8

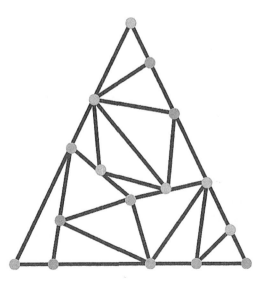

85. ▮▮▮▮▯

One of the following numbers is not divisible by any prime number less than 10.

Which is it?

(AMC 10B, 12B problem)

(A) $2^{1212} - 1$

(B) $2^{606} + 1$

(C) $2^{607} - 1$

(D) $2^{1213} - 1$

(E) $2^{1213} + 3^{1213}$

Solving Strategy

We need to check which of the given options is not divisible by any prime number less than 10. We can use modular arithmetic to eliminate the options one by one.

86.

N is chosen randomly from the set of integers between 1 and 2,040, inclusive.

What is the probability that the remainder when N^{20} is divided by 5 is 1?

(AMC 10B, 12B similar problem)

(A) $\dfrac{1}{5}$

(B) $\dfrac{3}{8}$

(C) $\dfrac{5}{8}$

(D) $\dfrac{4}{5}$

(E) $\dfrac{7}{8}$

87. ▰▰▰☐☐

The resulting sequence of four terms is obtained by adding each term of a four-term arithmetic sequence of positive integers to the corresponding term of a four-term geometric sequence of positive integers. The first three terms of the resulting sequence are 57, 60, and 91.

Determine the value of the fourth term of the resulting four-term sequence.

(AMC 10A problem)

(A)   202

(B)   204

(C)   206

(D)   208

(E)   300

🔢 Solving Strategy

First, we should write out the given sequence in terms of the arithmetic and geometric sequences. Then, we should use the given information to set up a system of equations and solve for the values of a, b, r, and d. Finally, we can use those values to find the fourth term of the resulting sequence.

88. ▪▪▪▫

A four-term sequence is formed by subtracting each term of a four-term geometric sequence of positive integers from the corresponding term of a four-term arithmetic sequence of positive integers. The first three terms of the resulting four-term sequence are 59, 34, and −15.

What is the fourth term of this sequence?

(AMC 10A similar problem)

(A) −136

(B) −122

(C) −114

(D) −108

(E) −90

89. ▮▮□□□

Consider an arithmetic sequence with a common difference of 2, and let S_n denote the sum of its first n terms. The quotient $\dfrac{S_{3n}}{S_n}$ does not depend on n.

What is the value of S_{30}?

(AMC 10B problem)

(A)   900

(B)   960

(C)   1000

(D)   1020

(E)   1060

Solving Strategy

For all values of n, the ratio of S_{3n} to S_n remains constant.

90. ■▢▢▢▢

How many terms are in the arithmetic sequence
15, 19, 23, ... , 75, 79 ?

(AMC 10B similar problem)

(A) 16

(B) 17

(C) 18

(D) 19

(E) 20

$$\begin{array}{r} 79 \\ -15 \\ \hline 64 \end{array}$$

16

91.

Among the first ten terms of the sequence 143, 11433, 1114333, ..., how many are prime numbers?

(AMC 10B, 12B problem)

(A) 0

(B) 1

(C) 2

(D) 3

(E) 4

Solving Strategy

Observe the pattern of the given sequence and find a general term for it. Use the general term to express the terms of the sequence and factorize them. Use the factorization to show that none of the terms are prime.

92. ◼◼◼☐☐

Suppose that a_n is an arithmetic sequence with
$a_1 + a_2 + \cdots + a_{100} = 200$ and $a_{101} + a_{102} + \cdots + a_{200} = 400$.

What is the value of $a_2 - a_1$?

(AMC 10B, 12B similar problem)

(A)   0.01

(B)   0.02

(C)   0.1

(D)   0.5

(E)   1

93. ◼◼◼◻◻

The data set contains 6 positive integers, which may not be distinct, and includes the value D among them: 2, 2, 5, 5, 6, and D. One of the 6 numbers in the data set is equal to the average (arithmetic mean) of the data set.

What is the sum of all positive integers that could replace D in order to satisfy the given conditions?

(AMC 10A, 12A problem)

(A)   24

(B)   26

(C)   28

(D)   30

(E)   32

$$20 + D = 6D$$
$$5D = 20$$
$$\frac{20 + D}{6} = 5 \quad D = 4$$
$$= D$$
$$D \approx 10$$
$$= 6$$
$$D = 16$$

🖩 Solving Strategy

First, we need to find the sum of the given integers. Then, we need to find the possible values of D by considering the fact that the average of the numbers is one of the values in the data set. Finally, we need to sum all positive values of X.

94. ■■■□□

A data set consists of 7 (not distinct) positive integers: 2, 8, 4, 4, 6, 6 and N. The average (arithmetic mean) of the 7 numbers equals a value in the data set.

What is the sum of all positive integers that could replace N in order to satisfy the given conditions?

(AMC 10A, 12A similar problem)

(A)   39

(B)   40

(C)   41

(D), 42

(E)   43

$$\frac{30 + N}{7} = 6$$

$$N = 12$$

$$= 4 \times$$

$$= 8$$

$$N = 26$$

$$= N$$

$$30 + N = 7N$$

$$8N = 30$$

$$N = 5$$

95. ▪▪▪□□

Doris writes down five positive integers. The unique mode of these integers is 3 greater than their median, and the median is 3 greater than their arithmetic mean.

What is the least possible value for the mode?

(AMC 10B, 12B problem)

(A)   11

(B)   12

(C)   13

(D)   14

(E)   15

$M + 3$

🖉 *Solving Strategy*

Let M be the median of the five positive integers. Since the unique mode is 3 greater than the median, the two largest integers are $M + 3$. Let a and b be the two smallest integers. We can use the fact that the median is 3 greater than the arithmetic mean to set up an equation relating x, y, and M. From there, we can minimize the sum $x + y$ to find the minimum value of the mode.

96. ▣▢▢▢▢

What is the sum of integers n for which the median of the numbers 3, 5, 7, 12, and n is equal to the mean of those five numbers?

(AMC 10B, 12B similar problem)

(A)   4

(B)   6

(C)   8

(D)   10

(E)   12

$$7 = \frac{27+n}{5} \quad n=8$$

$$5 = \frac{27+n}{5} \quad n=-2$$

$$n = \frac{27+n}{5}$$

$$5n = 27+n$$

$$4n = 27 \quad \times$$

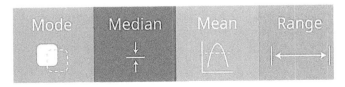

Assume that A is a subset of $\{1, 2, 3, \ldots, 25\}$ in which no element of A is equal to the sum of any two (not necessarily distinct) elements in A.

What is the maximum number of elements A may contain?

(AMC 10B problem)

(A)   11

(B)   13

(C)   21

(D)   23

(E)   25

—

Solving Strategy

To solve this question, we need to use some logical reasoning and constructive thinking. We can first try to set up some constraints based on the given condition and then construct a set that satisfies these constraints.

98. ■■□□□

Two subsets of the set $A = \{p, q, r, s, t\}$ are to be chosen so that their union is A and their intersection contains exactly two elements.

What is the number of ways to choose two subsets of the set $A = \{p, q, r, s, t\}$ such that their union is A and their intersection contains exactly two elements, where the order of choosing the subsets is not taken into account?

(AMC 10B similar problem)

(A)   10

(B)   20

(C)   30

(D)   40

(E)   50

99. ▮▮▮▯▯

Every school in a large school district is participating in a T-shirt fundraiser.

Which of the choices is the same logical meaning as the statement "No school bigger than Fermat School sold more T-shirts than Fermat School"?

(AMC 10B problem)

(A)   All schools that sold fewer T-shirts than Fermat School are smaller than Fermat School.

(B)   Every school that is smaller than Fermat School sold more T-shirts than Fermat School.

(C)   Every school that is bigger than Fermat School sold fewer T-shirts than Fermat School.

(D)   No school that sold more T-shirts than Fermat School is bigger than Fermat School.

(E)   Every school that is smaller than Fermat School sold fewer T-shirts than Fermat School sold.

Solving Strategy

To solve this problem, we need to understand the given statement logically and then find the statement that is equivalent to it. We can use two different methods to solve this problem. The first method involves converting the given statement into conditional statements and then finding the contrapositive of it. The second method involves considering a few schools and their T-shirt sales to eliminate the answer choices.

100. ▟▆☐☐☐

Mr. Simon promised that anyone who got all the open-ended questions right on the upcoming exam would receive an A on the exam.

Which one of these statements necessarily follows logically?

(AMC 10B similar problem)

(A)   If Tess did not receive an A, then she got all of the open-ended questions wrong.

(B)   If Tess did not receive an A, then she got at least one of the open-ended questions wrong.

(C)   If Tess received an A, then she got all of the open-ended questions right.

(D)   If Tess got at least one of the open-ended questions wrong, then she did not receive an A.

(E)   If Tess received an A, then she got at least one of the open-ended questions right.

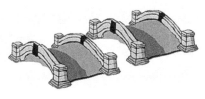

Question	Answer	Question	Answer
		76.	E
		77.	E
53.	C	78.	D
54.	C	79.	B
55.	D	80.	E
56.	C	81.	B
57.	C	82.	E
58.	E	83.	B
59.	D	84.	A
60.	B	85.	D
61.	E	86.	D
62.	D	87.	C
63.	C	88.	A
64.	C	89.	A
65.	B	90.	B
66.	C	91.	A
67.	C	92.	B
68.	E	93.	D
69.	C	94.	E
70.	B	95.	E
71.	E	96.	B
72.	D	97.	B
73.	A	98.	D
74.	A	99.	D
75.	C	100.	C

The top left section (A) can be painted in **5** possible colors. Then the bottom left section (B) can only be painted with **4** possible colors because it touches the top left section (A).

A	D	
B	C	E

The bottom middle section (C) can only be painted with **3** colors because it touches both the top left section (A) and the bottom left (B). There are **3** possible colors for the top right section (D) because it touches the top left section(A) but not the bottom left section (B).

There are **3** possible colors for the bottom right section (E) because it touches the bottom middle section (C) and the top right section (D) but not the top left section (A) or the bottom left section (B).

In summary,
A: 5 possible, B: 4 possible, C: 3 possible, D: 3possible, E: 3 possible coloring.
Using the counting principle, we can multiply the number of possible colors for each section to get the total number of possible colorings: $5 \times 4 \times 3 \times 3 \times 3 = 540$.
Therefore, there are 540 different colorings possible.

Starting at top left section (A):
can be painted in **4** possible colors
B: use different color at A so, **3** possible colors
C: use different color at B so, **3** possible colors
D: use different color at A and B so, **2** possible colors
E: use different color at D, B, and C so, **1** possible colors
F: use different color at E and C so, **2** possible colors
G: use different color at D and E so, **2** possible colors

In summary,
A: 4, B: 3, C: 3, D: 2, E: 3, F: 2, G: 2 possible coloring.

Using the counting principle, we can multiply the number of possible colors for each section to get the total number of possible colorings: $4 \times 3 \times 3 \times 2 \times 1 \times 2 \times 2 = 288$.

Therefore, there are 280 different colorings possible.

| 55. | **Answer** | (**D**) |

There are 8 possible equations

$$0 = 0 \ (1), \qquad x = 0 \ (2), \qquad y = 0 \ (3), \qquad z = 0 \ (4),$$
$$x + y = 0 \ (5), \qquad x + z = 0 \ (6), \qquad y + z = 0 \ (7),$$
$$x + y + z = 0 \ (8)$$

and we have to count the total number of systems of three linear equations with coefficients of 0 or 1. There are 2 choices for each coefficient, so there are $2^9 = 512$ possible systems. Note that no two equations by themselves can force $x = y = z = 0$, so we can exclude systems with equation (1) or repeated equations.

Case 1: equation (8), $x + y + z = 0$, is present.

① equation (8), and two equations from (5), (6), (7). There are $_3C_2 = 3$ ways to choose two equations from (5), (6), (7) and $3! = 6$ ways to arrange each case. The number of options that force $x = y = z = 0$ is $3 \times 3! = 18$. ② equation (8), one from (5), (6), (7), other from (2), (3), (4). There are $_3C_1 = 3$ ways to choose from (5), (6), (7). WLOG let us choose (7). Given $x + y + z = 0$ and $y + z = 0$, we conclude that $x = 0$. The third equation can be either $y = 0$ or $z = 0$. There are $3!$ ways to arrange each case. The number of options that force $x = y = z = 0$ is $3 \times 2 \times 3! = 36$. ③ equation (8), and two equations from (2), (3), (4). There are $_3C_2 = 3$ ways to choose two equations from (2), (3), (4) and $3! = 6$ ways to arrange each case. Each of these cases forces $x = y = z = 0$. $3 \times 3! = 18$ total options.

Case 2: equation (8) not present, at least one from (5), (6), (7) is present.

① equations (5), (6), (7) are all present. There are $3!$ ways to arrange the three equations. 6 options. ② two from (5), (6), (7), one equation from (2), (3), (4) is present. There are $_3C_2$ ways to choose two equations from (5), (6), (7). WLOG let (5) and (6) be in our system: $x + y = 0$ and $x+z=0$. Any equation from (2), (3), (4) will force $x = y = z = 0$. There are $3!$ ways to arrange the equations. The number of options that force $x = y = z = 0$ is $_3C_2 \times _3C_1 \times 3! = 54$. ③ one from (5), (6), (7) and two from (2), (3), (4) are present. There are $_3C_1$ ways to choose one from (5), (6), (7). WLOG let (5), $x + y = 0$, be present. One of the two from (2), (3), (4) must be (4), $z = 0$, since it is the only equation that restricts z. The last equation can be either (2) or (3). There are $3!$ ways to arrange the equations. The number of options that force $x = y = z = 0$ is $_3C_1 \times _2C_1 \times 3! = 36$.

Case 3: only equations (2), (3), (4) are present. There are $3!$ ways to arrange the three equations. 6 options.

We add up the cases: $18 + 36 + 18 + 6 + 54 + 36 + 6 = 174$ total systems force $x = y = z = 0$. Thus $512 - 174 = 338$.

56. **Answer** (C)

We need to find the number of four-digit positive integers that have at least one digit that is a 1 or a 5.

Let's first find the total number of four-digit integers:
The first digit cannot be 0, so we have 9 choices. For each of the remaining three digits, we have 10 choices (0 through 9). Therefore, the total number of four-digit integers is $9 \times 10 \times 10 \times 10 = 9,000$.

Now, let's find the number of four-digit integers that do not have any 1s or 5s as digits:
For the first digit, we still have 7 choices. For the remaining three digits, we only have 8 choices $(0, 2, 3, 4, 6, 7, 8, 9)$. Therefore, the total number of four-digit integers without any 1 or 5 is $7 \times 8 \times 8 \times 8 = 3584$.

Finally, we can find the number of four-digit integers that have at least one 1 or 5:
Subtract the number of four-digit integers without any 1 or 5 from the total number of four-digit integers: $9,000 - 3,584 = 5,416$.

Therefore, there are 5,416 integers.

57. **Answer** (C)

There are two cases to consider: (1) one even digit and two odd digits, and (2) three even digits.

For the first case, we can choose the odd digits in 5×5=25 ways and the even digit in 5 ways. There are three ways to order the even digit, so there are $25 \times 5 \times 3 = 375$ integers in this case. However, we need to subtract the number of integers that have 0 as the hundreds digit, which is $5 \times 5 = 25$, leaving us with 350 integers.

For the second case, we can choose each digit to be even in 5 ways, so there are $5 \times 5 \times 5 = 125$ integers in this case. However, we need to subtract the number of integers that have 0 as the hundreds digit, which is $5 \times 5 = 25$, leaving us with 100 integers.

Adding the two cases together, we get $350 + 100 = 450$ three-digit positive integers that have an odd number of even digits.

58. Answer (E)

The worst-case scenario is that we draw 10 socks of each of the three most populous colors: red, green, and yellow. This gives us a total of 10+10+10+10+8+6=54 socks without drawing 11 of any one color. Drawing one more socks will guarantee that we have drawn at least 11 socks of one color.

Therefore, we must draw 54+1=55 socks to guarantee that at least 55 socks of a single color will be drawn.

59. Answer (D)

Note that the integers from 8 through 14 must be in different pairs, and 7 must pair with 14. (7 and 14 pair → 1 way ①)

The number 6 can pair with either 12 or 13.
From here, we breaks down into two cases:
ⓐ case 1:
   If 6 and 12 form a pair (6 and 12 pair → 1 way ②) then,
   - 5 can be paired with one of the three numbers 10, 11, or 13 (5 and 10 or 5 and 11 or 5 and 13 pair → 3 ways ③).
   - If 5 is paired with 10,then
     4 must be paired with 8, 9, 11, or 13.
     That is, there are 4 number of ways for 4. (→ 4 ways ④)
   - In the same principle,
     in case of 3, the number of choices is reduced to 3, so there are 3 number of ways (→ 3 ways ⑤),
     2 has 2 number of ways (→ 2 ways ⑥), and
     1 has 1 number of ways (→ 1 ways ⑦).
So, there are
$$① × ② × ③ × ④ × ⑤ × ⑥ × ⑦ = 1 × 1 × 3 × 4 × 3 × 2 × 1$$
$$= 3 × 4! \text{ ways in the case1.}$$
ⓑ case 2:
   If 6 and 13 form a pair (6 and 13 pair → 1 way) then,
   - 5 can be paired with one of the three numbers 10, 11, or 12 (5 and 10 or 5 and 11 or 5 and 12 pair → 3 ways).
   The numbers 4, 3, 2, and 1 have the same number of ways as case 1.
   So, case 2 has the same total number of ways (3 × 4!) as case 1.

Therefore, number of ways is ⓐ or ⓑ
$$= ⓐ+ⓑ = 3 × 4! + 3 × 4! = 2 × 3 × 4! = 6 × 4!.$$

60. **Answer** **(B)**

Note that the side lengths from 9 through 16 must be in different pairs, and 8 must pair with 16. (8 and 16 pair → 1 way ①)

The side length 7 can pair with either 14 or 15.
From here, we breaks down into two cases:
ⓐ case 1:
  If 7 and 14 form a pair (7 and 14 pair → 1 way ②) then,
  - 6 can be paired with one of the three side lengths 12, 13, or 15 (6 and 12 or 6 and 13 or 6 and 15 pair → 3 ways ③).
  - If 6 is paired with 12,then
    5 can be paired with one of the four side lengths 10, 11, 13. or 15 (→ 4 ways ④).
  - Now, the remaining numbers greater than 8 are **9, 11, 13, 15** and the remaining numbers less than 5 are **4, 3, 2, 1**.
    4 must be paired with 9, 11, 13, or 15.
    That is, there are 4 number of ways for 4. (→ 4 ways ⑤)
  - Now, - In the same principle,
    in case of 3, the number of choices is reduced to 3, so there are 3 number of ways (→ 3 ways ⑥),
    2 has 2 number of ways (→ 2 ways ⑦), and
    1 has 1 number of ways (→ 1 ways ⑧).
So, there are
$$① \times ② \times ③ \times ④ \times ⑤ \times ⑥ \times ⑦ \times ⑧$$
$$= 1 \times 1 \times 3 \times 4 \times 4 \times 3 \times 2 \times 1$$
$$= 3 \times 4 \times 4! \text{ ways in the case1.}$$
ⓑ case 2:
  If 7 and 15 form a pair (7 and 15 pair → 1 way) then,
  - 6 can be paired with one of the three numbers 12, 13, or 14
    numbers 5, 4, 3, 2, and 1 have the same number of ways as case 1.
  So, case 2 has the same total number of ways ($3 \times 4 \times 4!$) as case 1.

Therefore, number of ways is ⓐ or ⓑ
$$= ⓐ + ⓑ$$
$$= 3 \times 4 \times 4! + 3 \times 4 \times 4! = 288 + 288 = 576$$

| 61. | **Answer** | **(E)** |

We are given 13 cards numbered from 1 to 13. We need to find the number of ways to arrange them such that exactly two passes are required to pick up all the cards in increasing order.

Let us assume that k cards are picked up in the first pass, where $1 \le k \le 12$. This means that the remaining $13 - k$ cards will be picked up in the second pass.

Once we pick the spots for the k cards on the first pass, there is only one way to arrange all 13 cards. The number of ways to choose k spots from 13 spots is $_{13}C_K$. However, we need to exclude the arrangement in which all 13 cards are picked up in the first pass. This is because we are interested in exactly two passes. Therefore, the number of ways to pick k spots is ($_{13}C_K - 1$).

The remaining $13 - k$ cards will be picked up in the second pass, and there is only one way to arrange them. Therefore, the total number of ways to arrange the cards such that exactly two passes are required is given by the sum of ($_{13}C_k - 1$) for $k = 1$ to 12.

So, the sum is:

$$\sum_{k=1}^{12} (\ _{13}C_k - 1) = \sum_{k=1}^{12} \ _{13}C_k - 12$$

Using binomial expansion

$$\sum_{k=1}^{12} \ _{13}C_k = \ _{13}C_1 + \ _{13}C_2 + \ _{13}C_3 + \dots + \ _{13}C_{12}$$
$$= (\ _{13}C_0 + \ _{13}C_1 + \ _{13}C_2 + \dots + \ _{13}C_{13}) - \ _{13}C_0 - \ _{13}C_{13}$$
$$= (1 + 1)^{13} - 2 = 2^{13} - 2$$

Therefore the answer is $2^{13} - 2 - 12 = 8192 - 14 = 8178$.

| 62. | *Answer* | (**D**) |

We are given 10 cards numbered from 1 to 10. We need to find the number of ways to arrange them such that exactly two passes are required to pick up all the cards in increasing order.
Let us assume that k cards are picked up in the first pass, where $1 \leq k \leq 9$. This means that the remaining $10 - k$ cards will be picked up in the second pass.

Once we pick the spots for the k cards on the first pass, there is only one way to arrange all 10 cards. The number of ways to choose k spots from 10 spots is $_{10}C_K$. However, we need to exclude the arrangement in which all 10 cards are picked up in the first pass. This is because we are interested in exactly two passes. Therefore, the number of ways to pick k spots is ($_{10}C_K - 1$).

The remaining $10 - k$ cards will be picked up in the second pass, and there is only one way to arrange them. Therefore, the total number of ways to arrange the cards such that exactly two passes are required is given by the sum of ($_{10}C_k - 1$) for $k = 1$ to 10.

So, the sum is:

$$\sum_{k=1}^{9} (\,_{10}C_k - 1) = \sum_{k=1}^{9} \,_{10}C_k - 9$$

Using binomial expansion

$$\sum_{k=1}^{9} \,_{10}C_k = \,_{10}C_1 + \,_{10}C_2 + \,_{10}C_3 + ... + \,_{10}C_9$$
$$= (\,_{10}C_0 + \,_{10}C_1 + \,_{10}C_2 + ... + \,_{10}C_{10}) - \,_{10}C_0 - \,_{10}C_{10}$$
$$= (1 + 1)^{10} - 2 = 2^{10} - 2$$

Therefore the answer is $2^{10} - 2 - 9 = 1024 - 11 = 1013$.

| 63. | *Answer* | (C) |

According to the problem, a string is valid if for each $n = \{1,2,3,4\}$, at least n of the digits are less than n. We can use this rule to deduce what kind of strings are valid. For example, since 0 is less than 1, every valid string must have at least one 0. Next, we can perform casework on the number of different digits such strings can have. We can compute the number of strings in each case by using permutations.

1) string has 1 digit only possibility is 00000
    → there is 1 string
2) string has 2 different digits $(01, 02, 03, 04$ cases)
    ① 00001/ 00002/ 00003/ 00004 cases → $4 \times \frac{5!}{4!} = 20$
    ② 00011/ 00022/ 00033 cases → $3 \times \frac{5!}{3! \times 2!} = 30$
    ③ 00111/ 00222 cases → $2 \times \frac{5!}{2! \times 3!} = 20$
    ④ 01111 cases → $1 \times \frac{5!}{4!} = 5$
    → so, there is $20 + 30 + 20 + 5 = 75$ strings
3) string has 3 different digits $(012, 013, 014, 023, 024, 034$ cases)
    ① 00012/ 00013/ 00014/ 00023/ 00024/ 00034 → $6 \times \frac{5!}{3!} = 120$
    ② 00112/ 00113/ 00114/ 00223/ 00224 cases → $5 \times \frac{5!}{2! \times 2!} = 150$
    ③ 00122/ 00133/ 00233 cases → $3 \times \frac{5!}{2! \times 2!} = 90$
    ④ 01112/ 01113/ 01114 cases → $3 \times \frac{5!}{3!} = 60$
    ⑤ 01122/ 01133 cases → $2 \times \frac{5!}{2! \times 2!} = 60$
    ⑥ 01222 cases → $1 \times \frac{5!}{3!} = 20$
    → so, there is $120 + 150 + 90 + 60 + 60 + 20 = 500$ strings
4) string has 4 different digits $(0123, 0124, 0134, 0234$ cases)
    ① 00123/ 00124/ 00134/ 00234 cases → $4 \times \frac{5!}{2!} = 240$
    ② 01123/ 01124/ 01134 cases → $3 \times \frac{5!}{2!} = 180$
    ③ 01223/ 01224 cases → $2 \times \frac{5!}{2!} = 120$
    ④ 01233 cases → $1 \times \frac{5!}{2!} = 60$
    → so, there is $240 + 180 + 120 + 60 = 600$ strings
5) string has 5 different digits $(01234$ case)
    → there is $5! = 120$ strings

Therefore, there is $1 + 75 + 500 + 600 + 120 = 1296$ strings.

64. **Answer** (*C*)

There are 4 choices for the first element of N, and for each of these choices there are 4! ways to arrange the remaining elements. If the second element must be 2, then there are only 3 choices for the first element and 3! ways to arrange the remaining elements.

Hence the answer is $\dfrac{3 \times 3!}{4 \times 4!} = \dfrac{18}{96} = \dfrac{3}{16}$, and $x + y = 19$.

65. **Answer** (*B*)

To solve this problem, we need to use geometric probability. We can find the probability that any number of randomly distributed numbers on the interval $[0, 1]$ sum to more than 1 using geometric probability. In the first case, when we have two variables x and y, we graph the points that satisfy $x + y < 1$, $0 < x, y < 1$, which gives us the triangle with points $(0, 0), (1, 0)$, and $(0, 1)$. The probability of this case happening is simply the area of the triangle divided by the total area of the graph, which is always 1.

Therefore, $P(x + y \leq 1) = \dfrac{\frac{1}{2} \times 1^2}{1^2} = \dfrac{1}{2}$.

In the second case, when we have three variables x, y, and z, we graph the points that satisfy $x + y + z < 1$, $0 < x, y, z < 1$, which gives us the tetrahedron with points $(0, 0, 0)$, $(1, 0, 0)$, $(0, 1, 0)$, and $(0, 0, 1)$. The probability of this case happening is simply the volume of the tetrahedron divided by the total volume of the graph, which is always 1.

Therefore, $P(x + y + z \leq 1) = \dfrac{\frac{1}{3} \times (\frac{1}{2} \times 1^2) \times 1}{1^3} = \dfrac{1}{6}$.

Next, we consider the two cases where Frederick takes exactly two or three steps. For the first case, we need $x_1 + x_2 > 1$ and $t_1 + t_2 > 1$. This means that the sum of the distances that Frederick jumps in the first two steps is greater than 1, and the sum of the times that Frederick takes to jump in the first two steps is greater than 1 minute. The probability of this happening is $P(x_1 + x_2 > 1) \times P(t_1 + t_2 > 1)$, where x_1 and x_2 are independently and uniformly distributed in the interval $(0,1)$ and so are t_1 and t_2. We know that $P(x_1 + x_2 > 1) = \dfrac{1}{2}$, and $P(t_1 + t_2 > 1) = \dfrac{1}{2}$, so the probability of this case happening is $\dfrac{1}{4}$. (1)

For the second case, we need $x_1 + x_2 + x_3 > 1$ and $t_1 + t_2 \leq 1$. This means that the sum of the distances that Frederick jumps in all three steps is greater than 1, and the sum of the times that Frederick takes to jump in the first two steps is less than or equal to 1 minute. The probability of this happening is $P(x_1 + x_2 + x_3 > 1) \times P(t_1 + t_2 \leq 1)$, where x_1, x_2, and x_3 are independently and uniformly distributed in the interval $(0,1)$, and so are t_1 and t_2. We know that $P(x_1 + x_2 + x_3 > 1) = \frac{5}{6}$, and $P(t_1 + t_2 \leq 1) = \frac{1}{2}$, so the probability of this case happening is $\frac{5}{12}$.

Therefore, the total probability of Frederick's position being greater than 1 is $\frac{1}{4} + \frac{5}{12} = \frac{2}{3}$.

---

66. **Answer**   (**C**)

We consider three cases based on where the second point is chosen: on the same side (P_1) as the first point (P_0), on an adjacent side (P_2), or on the opposite side (P_3). The probabilities of these events are $\frac{1}{4}$, $\frac{1}{2}$, and $\frac{1}{4}$, respectively, given that the first point is chosen on a fixed side.

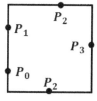

Case 1) The two points lie on the same side. Assume that there are two points a and b on the x-axis, where a and b are between 0 and 1 inclusive. Consider (a, b) a point on the unit square $[0,1] \times [0,1]$ on the Cartesian plane. The area of the set $\{(a,b): |b - a| > \frac{1}{2}\}$ is equal to $\left(\frac{1}{2}\right)^2 = \frac{1}{4}$.

Case 2) The two points are situated on two adjacent sides. Let the two sides be $[0,1]$ on the x-axis and $[0,1]$ on the y-axis and let one point be $(a, 0)$ and the other point be $(0, b)$. As in Case 1, (a, b) is a point on the unit square $[0,1] \times [0,1]$. The area of the region $\{(a,b): \sqrt{a^2 + b^2} \leq \frac{1}{2}, \ 0 \leq a, b \leq 1\}$ is $\frac{\pi}{16}$ and the area of its complementary set inside the square (i.e. $\{(a,b): \sqrt{a^2 + b^2} > \frac{1}{2}, \ 0 \leq a, b \leq 1\}$) is $1 - \frac{\pi}{16}$. Therefore, the probability that the distance between $(a, 0)$ and $(0, b)$ is at least $\frac{1}{2}$ is $1 - \frac{\pi}{16}$.

Case 3) Two points are on two opposite sides. In this case, the probability that the distance between the two points is at least $\frac{1}{2}$ is obviously 1.

Thus the probability that the probability that the distance between the two points is at least $\frac{1}{2}$ is given by;

$$\left(\frac{1}{4}\right) \times \left(\frac{1}{4}\right) + \left(\frac{1}{2}\right) \times \left(1 - \frac{\pi}{16}\right) + (1) \times \left(\frac{1}{4}\right) = \frac{26 - \pi}{32}.$$

Therefore $x = 26, y = -1$, and $z = 32$. Thus, $x + y + z = 57$.

| 67. | *Answer* | (C)

The probability of getting a sum of 5 on one roll of two dice is $\frac{4}{36}$, or $\frac{1}{9}$, since there are four ways to roll a sum of 5: $(1,4), (2,3), (3,2)$, and $(4,1)$, out of 36 possible outcomes.

The complement of getting a sum of 5 is not getting a sum of 5, which has a probability of $1 - \frac{1}{9} = \frac{8}{9}$. The probability of getting a sum of 5 at least once in n rolls is equal to 1 minus the probability of not getting a sum of 5 in n rolls, which is $\left(\frac{8}{9}\right)^n$. We want this probability to be greater than 1/2, so we can set up the inequality:

$$1 - \left(\frac{8}{9}\right)^n > \frac{1}{2}.$$

Simplifying this inequality gives:

$$\left(\frac{8}{9}\right)^n < \frac{1}{2}$$

Taking the logarithm of both sides with base $\frac{8}{9}$ or

$$\left(\frac{8}{9}\right)^6 < \frac{1}{2} < \left(\frac{8}{9}\right)^5.$$

The least integer n satisfying the inequality is 6.

68. Answer (E)

We split this problem into 2 cases.

Case 1: All four dice show the same value.

There are 6 ways (1 or 2 or 3 or 4 or 5 or 6) to choose the value that all four dice will show. After the first dice is rolled, the probability that each of the remaining three dice will show the same value is 1/6. Therefore, the probability that all four dice show the same value is:

$$6 \times \frac{1}{6} \times \frac{1}{6} \times \frac{1}{6} \times \frac{1}{6} = \frac{1}{216}.$$

Case 2: Three dice show the same value and the fourth shows a different value.

There are 6 ways (1 or 2 or 3 or 4 or 5 or 6) to choose the value that will appear on the three dice that show the same value. There are also 4 ways ($_4C_3 = 4$) to choose which of the three dice will show the same value.

After the first dice is rolled, the probability that the second dice will show the same value as the first dice is 1/6. The probability that the third dice will also show the same value is also 1/6. Finally, the probability that the fourth dice will show a different value is 5/6. Therefore, the probability that three dice show the same value and the fourth shows a different value is:

$$6 \times 4 \times \frac{1}{6} \times \frac{1}{6} \times \frac{1}{6} \times \frac{5}{6} = \frac{5}{54}.$$

Adding these up, we get;

$$\frac{1}{216} + \frac{5}{54} = \frac{7}{72}.$$

69. Answer (C)

To find the prime factorization of n, we first note that the prime factorization of 18 is 2×3^2 and 180 is $2^2 \times 3^2 \times 5$.

Since the LCM of n and 18 is 180,

the prime factorization of n must have

      factor 2 raised to the power of 2,

      factor 3 raised to the power of at most 2, and

      factor 5 raised to the power of 1.

To find the prime factorization of n, we second note that the prime factorization of 45 is $3^2 \times 5$ and 15 is 3×5.

Since the GCF of n and 45 is 15, n must have

      a factor of 3 raised to the power of 1 and

      a factor of 5 raised to the power of 1.

Therefore, we can write n as $2^2 \times 3 \times 5 = 60$.

70. Answer (B)

We first note that the prime factorization of the four numbers
$$30 = 2 \times 3 \times 5$$
$$240 = 2^4 \times 3 \times 5$$
$$60 = 2^2 \times 3 \times 5$$
$$20 = 2^2 \times 5$$

Since the LCM of m and 30 is 240, the prime factorization of m must have
> factor 2 raised to the power of 4
> factor 3 raised to the power of 0 or 1
> factor 5 raised to the power of 0 or 1

Since the GCD of m and 60 is 20, m must have
> factor 2 raised to the power of at least 2
> factor 3 raised to the power of 0
> factor 5 raised to the power of 1

Therefore, we can write n as $2^4 \times 5 = 80$ and the sum of the digits of 80 is 8+0=8.

71. Answer (E)

Let $0.\overline{pqr}$ be x. So,
$$x = 0.pqrpqr \ldots \text{ (1)}$$
$$1000x = pqr.pqrpqr \ldots \text{(2)}$$
(2)-(1) $999x = pqr \quad \rightarrow \quad x = \dfrac{pqr}{999} \quad \rightarrow 0.\overline{pqr} = \dfrac{100p+10q+r}{999}.$

Similarly,
$$0.\bar{p} = \frac{p}{9}, \qquad 0.\bar{q} = \frac{q}{9}, \qquad 0.\bar{r} = \frac{r}{9}$$

From the given condition;
$$0.\overline{pqr} = \frac{1}{3}(0.\bar{p} + 0.\bar{q} + 0.\bar{r})$$
$$\frac{100p + 10q + r}{999} = \frac{1}{3}\left(\frac{p}{9} + \frac{q}{9} + \frac{r}{9}\right)$$
$$100p + 10q + r = 37p + 37q + 37r$$
$$63p = 27q + 36r$$
$$7p = 3q + 4r$$

From p, q, and r are digits and sum of coefficients is $7 = 3 + 4$;
① case 1: $p = q = r$
there are 9 possible solutions: (1,1,1), (2,2,2), ..., (9,9,9).

② case 2: $p \neq q \neq r$
    In this case, satisfy the following conditions:
        q increases by 4 as r decreases by 3, or
        q decreases by 4 as r increases by 3.
    Using this information, we can find possible solutions:
    there are 4 possible solutions: (4,8,1), (5,1,8), (5,9,2), (9,9,9).

Therefore, the number of distinct sets of three nonzero digits
is 9+4=13.

---

71. **Answer**   (**E**)

Let $0.\overline{pqr}$ be x. So,
$$x = 0.pqrpqr \ldots \quad (1)$$
$$1000x = pqr.pqrpqr \ldots (2)$$
(2)-(1) $999x = pqr \quad \rightarrow \quad x = \dfrac{pqr}{999} \quad \rightarrow 0.\overline{pqr} = \dfrac{100p+10q+r}{999}.$

Similarly,
$$0.\bar{p} = \frac{p}{9}, \qquad 0.\bar{q} = \frac{q}{9}, \qquad 0.\bar{r} = \frac{r}{9}$$

From the given condition;
$$0.\overline{pqr} = \frac{1}{3}(0.\bar{p} + 0.\bar{q} + 0.\bar{r})$$
$$\frac{100p + 10q + r}{999} = \frac{1}{3}\left(\frac{p}{9} + \frac{q}{9} + \frac{r}{9}\right)$$
$$100p + 10q + r = 37p + 37q + 37r$$
$$63p = 27q + 36r$$
$$7p = 3q + 4r$$

From $p, q,$ and r are digits and sum of coefficients is $7 = 3 + 4$;
① case 1: $p = q = r$
    there are 9 possible solutions: (1,1,1), (2,2,2), ..., (9,9,9).
② case 2: $p \neq q \neq r$
    In this case, satisfy the following conditions:
        q increases by 4 as r decreases by 3, or
        q decreases by 4 as r increases by 3.
    Using this information, we can find possible solutions:
    there are 4 possible solutions: (4,8,1), (5,1,8), (5,9,2), (9,9,9).

Therefore, the number of distinct sets of three nonzero digits
is 9+4=13.

72. **Answer** **(D)**

Let's denote the repeating decimal 4.xyxy... as a fraction using the definition of repeating decimals and making an equation.

$$44 \times 4.xy = 44 \times (4.xyxy\,....) - 0.4$$
$$44 \times (4.xyxy\,...) - 44 \times (4.xy) = 0.4$$
$$44 \times (4.xyxy\,... - 4.xy) = 0.4$$
$$44 \times (0.00xy\,...) = 0.4$$
$$44 \times \left(\frac{1}{100}\right) \times (0.xyxy\,....) = 0.4$$
$$0.xyxy\,... = \frac{10}{11}$$

Using division;
$$10 \div 11 = 0.909090\,....$$

Therefore, $x = 9, y = 0$ and the number is 90.

73. **Answer** **(A)**

Let the two primes be a and b $(a > b)$. We know that $a - b = 2$ and $a^3 - b^3 = 62426$.

Using the difference of cubes formula, we have
$$(a - b)(a^2 + ab + b^2) = a^3 - b^3 = 62426.$$
Substituting $a - b = 2$, we get $2(a^2 + ab + b^2) = 62426$.
Simplifying, we get $a^2 + ab + b^2 = 31213$.

Let's introduce another variable. Instead of using a and b, we can express the primes as $x + 2$ and x, where a is $x + 2$ and b is x.
Substituting $x + 2$ for a and x for b, we get
$$(x + 2)^2 + x(x + 2) + x^2 = 3x^2 + 6x + 4 = 31213.$$
Then we subtract 4 from both sides to get $3x^2 + 6x = 31209$.

Notice how if we had 1 to both sides, the left side would become a perfect square trinomial:
$$x^2 + 2x + 1 = 10404 \text{ which is } (x + 1)^2 = 10404.$$
The two primes a and b must be odd, therefore $x + 1$ is the number in the middle of them.

$10404 = 102^2$ so the two numbers are 101 and 103.
The next prime number is 107, and $1 + 0 + 7 = 8$ so the answer is 8.

74. **Answer** (*A*)

17391 can be expressed as $17408 - 17 = 17391$ so,
$$17391 = 17 \times (2^{10} - 1).$$

Using the difference of squares formula,
we can write $2^{10} - 1$ as $(2^5 + 1) \times (2^5 - 1)$.
Thus, $17391 = 17 \times (2^5 + 1) \times (2^5 - 1)$
$$= 17 \times 33 \times 31.$$

Since 33 is composite, the greatest prime factor of 17,391 is 31.
The sum of the digits of 31 is $3 + 1 = 4$.

75. **Answer** (*C*)

We want to count the number of sets that contain exactly two multiples of 7.
Case 1: The multiples of 7 are 1 (mod 10) and 8 (mod 10). That is, the first and eighth elements of such sets are multiples of 7. The first element is $1 + 10k$ for some integer $0 \leq k \leq 99$. It is a multiple of 7 when $k = 2, 9, 16, \ldots, 93$.
Explain in detail:
The first element of each set is of the form $1 + 10k$, where k is an integer between 0 and 99. To be a multiple of 7, the first element must be of the form 7n, where n is an integer. Thus, we need to find the values of k for which $1 + 10k$ is of the form 7n.
To simplify this task, we can look at the remainders of $1+10k$ when divided by 7.
Case 2: The multiples of 7 are 2 (mod 10) and 9 (mod 10). That is, the second and ninth elements of such sets are multiples of 7. The second element is $2 + 10k$ for some integer $0 \leq k \leq 99$. It is a multiple of 7 when $k = 4, 11, 18, \ldots, 95$.
Case 3: The multiples of 7 are 3 (mod 10) and 0 (mod 10). That is, the third and tenth elements of such sets are multiples of 7. The third element is $3 + 10k$ for some integer $0 \leq k \leq 99$.
It is a multiple of 7 when $k = 6, 13, 20, \ldots, 97$.

Note that each case has $[\frac{100}{7}] = 14$ sets. Therefore, the answer is simply the product of the number of cases and the number of sets per case, which is $14 \times 3 = 42$.

76. Answer (E)

The problem asks to find the possible value of $S(n + 1)$ given that $S(n)$ equals 2065, where $S(n)$ is defined as the sum of the digits of a positive integer n.

First, we note that if the sum of the digits of a number is a multiple of 9, then the number itself is also a multiple of 9. Also, the sum of the digits of a number is congruent to the number itself modulo 9.

Therefore, since S(n) equals 2065, which is not a multiple of 9, n is not a multiple of 9 either. Using the fact that S(n) is congruent to n modulo 9, we can see that n is congruent to 4 modulo 9.

Hence, $n + 1$ is congruent to 5 modulo 9, and the only answer choice that satisfies this condition is (E) 5459. Therefore, the possible value of $S(n + 1)$ is $5 + 4 + 5 + 9 = 23 \equiv 5 \ (mod \ 9)$.

77. Answer (E)

We'll use the first approach and simplify the nested fraction first. Starting from the inside, we have:

$$\cfrac{1}{3 + \cfrac{1}{3}} = \cfrac{1}{\cfrac{9+1}{3}} = \cfrac{1}{\cfrac{10}{3}} = \cfrac{3}{10}$$

Substituting this into the original expression gives:

$$3 + \cfrac{1}{3 + \cfrac{3}{10}} = 3 + \cfrac{1}{\cfrac{33}{10}} = 3 + \cfrac{10}{33} = \cfrac{99 + 10}{33} = \cfrac{109}{33}$$

So the value of the expression is $\cfrac{109}{33}$.

78. Answer (D)

We'll use the first approach and simplify the nested fraction first. Starting from the inside, we have:

$$\cfrac{1}{5 + \cfrac{1}{5}} = \cfrac{1}{\cfrac{25+1}{5}} = \cfrac{1}{\cfrac{26}{5}} = \cfrac{5}{26}$$

Substituting this into the original expression gives:

$$5 + \cfrac{1}{5 + \cfrac{5}{26}} = 5 + \cfrac{1}{\cfrac{135}{26}} = 5 + \cfrac{26}{135} = \cfrac{675 + 26}{135} = \cfrac{701}{135}$$

So the value of the expression is $\cfrac{701}{135}$.

79. **Answer** **(B)**

To solve this problem, we need to find the smallest positive integer that is divisible by all integers from 1 to 17.

This is given by the least common multiple (LCM) of all integers from 1 to 17, which can be found by prime factorizing each integer and taking the highest power of each prime factor. Thus, we get $S_{17} = 2^4 \times 3^2 \times 5 \times 7 \times 11 \times 13 \times 17 = 16 \times 9 \times 5 \times 7 \times 11 \times 13 \times 17$.

Next, we need to simplify the given expression using S_{17} and modular arithmetic to find the remainder when k is divided by 17.

Multiplying the denominators by S_{17} gives:

$$\frac{1}{1} + \frac{1}{2} + \frac{1}{3} + \ldots + \frac{1}{17} = \frac{k}{S_{17}}$$

$$k = \frac{1}{1} \times S_{17} + \frac{1}{2} \times S_{17} + \frac{1}{3} \times S_{17} + \ldots + \frac{1}{17} \times S_{17}$$

Since S_{17} is a multiple of 17, all terms except the last one will be a multiple of 17. Thus, the remainder of all other terms when divided by 17 will be 0. Therefore, the problem is essentially asking us what the remainder of $\frac{1}{17} \times S_{17}$ is when divided by 17. This can be found by simplifying the expression using modular arithmetic as follows:

$$\frac{S_{17}}{17} \pmod{17} = (16) \times (9) \times (5) \times (7) \times (11) \times (13) \times \pmod{17}$$

$$= (-1) \times (9) \times (5) \times (7) \times (11) \times (13) \times \pmod{17}$$
$$= (-1) \times (9) \times (35) \times (11) \times (13) \times \pmod{17}$$
$$= (-1) \times (9) \times (1) \times (11) \times (13) \times \pmod{17}$$
$$= (9) \times (11) \times (-13) \times \pmod{17}$$
$$= (9) \times (11) \times (4) \times \pmod{17}$$
$$= (36) \times (11) \times \pmod{17}$$
$$= (2) \times (11) \times \pmod{17}$$
$$= (22) \times \pmod{17}$$
$$= 5$$

Therefore the remainder is 5.

80.	**Answer**	**(E)**

To solve this problem, we need to find the smallest positive integer that is divisible by all integers from 1 to 13.

This is given by the least common multiple (LCM) of all integers from 1 to 13, which can be found by prime factorizing each integer and taking the highest power of each prime factor. Thus, we get $C_{13} = 2^3 \times 3^2 \times 5 \times 7 \times 11 \times 13 = 8 \times 9 \times 5 \times 7 \times 11 \times 13$.

Next, we need to simplify the given expression using C_{13} and modular arithmetic to find the remainder when k is divided by 13.

Multiplying the denominators by C_{13} gives:
$$\frac{1}{2} + \frac{1}{3} + \frac{1}{4} \ ... + \frac{1}{13} = \frac{k}{C_{13}}$$
$$k = \frac{1}{2} \times C_{13} + \frac{1}{3} \times C_{13} + \frac{1}{4} \times C_{13} + \ ... + \frac{1}{13} \times C_{13}$$

Since C_{13} is a multiple of 13, all terms except the last one will be a multiple of 13. Thus, the remainder of all other terms when divided by 13 will be 0. Therefore, the problem is essentially asking us what the remainder of $\frac{1}{13} \times C_{13}$ is when divided by 13. This can be found by simplifying the expression using modular arithmetic as follows:

$$\frac{C_{13}}{13} (mod\ 13) = (8) \times (9) \times (5) \times (7) \times (11) \times (mod\ 13)$$
$$= (8) \times (-4) \times (5) \times (7) \times (-2) \times (mod\ 13)$$
$$= (8) \times (8) \times (5) \times (7) \times (mod\ 13)$$
$$= (-5) \times (-5) \times (5) \times (7) \times (mod\ 13)$$
$$= (10) \times (35) \times (mod\ 13)$$
$$= (10) \times (9) \times (mod\ 13)$$
$$= (-3) \times (-4) \times (mod\ 13)$$
$$= (12) \times (mod\ 13)$$
$$= 12$$

Therefore the remainder is 12.

Let A, B, and C be the squares with the number of lattice points a, b, and c, respectively. Note that the actual lengths of the side lengths are the number of lattice points minus 1 and the number of lattice points inside a rectangular region is equal to the number of lattice points in its width times the number of lattice points along its length.

Using this fact, the number of lattice points in A is a^2, the number of lattice points in B is b^2, and the number of lattice points in C is c^2. Having satisfied the first condition,

$$a^2 = \frac{9}{4}b^2 \quad \rightarrow \quad a = \frac{3}{2}b \quad (1)$$

→ another meaning of this expression is that s is a multiple of 2.

C contains $\frac{1}{4}$ of the number of lattice points contained in $A \cup B$, which can be calculated by adding the number of lattice points in the bounded regions of A and B, excluding the lattice points along the y-axis for the full length of B, and dividing the result by 4.

$$c^2 = \frac{1}{4}(a^2 + b^2 - b) \rightarrow c^2 = \frac{1}{4}\left(\frac{9}{4}b^2 + b^2 - b\right) \rightarrow 16c^2 = 13b^2 - 4b$$

$$\rightarrow 16c^2 = b(13b - 4) \quad (2)$$

The fraction of the lattice points inside B that are inside $B \cap C$ is 27 times the fraction of lattice points inside a that are inside $A \cap C$. If x is the number of lattice points formed by $B \cap C$ and y is the number of lattice points formed by $A \cap C$, then the number of lattice points in $B \cap C$ is xc and the number of lattice points in $A \cap C$ is yc.

So,

$$\frac{xc}{b^2} = 27 \times \frac{yc}{a^2} \quad \rightarrow \quad \frac{x}{b^2} = \frac{y}{\frac{9}{4} \times b^2} \quad \rightarrow \quad x = 12y$$

thus,

$$c = x + y - 1 \quad \rightarrow \quad c = 12y + y - 1 \quad \rightarrow \quad c = 13y - 1.$$

Using modular arithmetic;

$$c \equiv -1 \ (mod \ 13) \quad \rightarrow \quad c^2 \equiv 1 \ (mod \ 13)$$

And from (2) $16 \times 1 \equiv b \times (-4) \ (mod \ 13) \quad \rightarrow \quad b \equiv -4 \ (mod \ 13)$.

So, $a \equiv \frac{3}{2}(-4) \equiv -6 \ (mod \ 13)$ and $a + b + c \equiv -11 \equiv 2 \ (mod \ 13)$.

Actual lengths of the side lengths are $a - 1$, $b - 1$, and $c - 1$ so, the sum of side length is $a + b + c - 3 \equiv -1 \ (mod \ 13)$.

Therefore, from the given example answer, the correct answer is 389 ($= 29 \times 13 + 12$).

| 82. | **Answer** | (**E**) |

Note that for any integer a, we have $n \equiv n^3 \pmod 6$. This is true because $n^3 - n = n(n-1)(n+1)$ is always divisible by 2 and 3. Thus, n and n^3 have the same remainders when divided by 2 and 3, and hence by the Chinese Remainder Theorem, they have the same remainder when divided by 6. For example, $4 = 4^3 \pmod 6$ because $4 - 4^3 = -60$ is divisible by 6.

Therefore, $n_1 + n_2 + \ldots + n_{2022} \pmod 6$

is congruent to $n_1^3 + n_2^3 + \ldots + n_{2022}^3 \pmod 6$.

This is because each term in the sum has the same remainder as its cube when divided by 6, by the observation above.

So,

the answer is congruent to $2022^{2022} \equiv 2^{2022} \pmod 6 = 4$. To see this, note that $2^n \pmod 6$ alternates between 2 and 4 as n increases. Specifically, $2^1 \pmod 6 \equiv 2$, $2^2 \pmod 6 \equiv 4$, $2^3 \pmod 6 \equiv 2$, $2^4 \pmod 6 \equiv 4$, and so on. Thus, we can write $2^{2022} \pmod 6 \equiv 2^{(2*1011)} \pmod 6 \equiv (2^2)^{1011} \pmod 6 \equiv 4^{1011} \pmod 6 = 4 \pmod 6$.

Therefore, the remainder when $n_1^3 + n_2^3 + \ldots + n_{2022}^3$ is divided by 6 is 4.

83. **Answer** **(B)**

Let's start by using the given expression in terms of S_n:

$$a_{2019} + 2a_{2020} + 4a_{2021} + 8a_{2022} = \frac{S_{2023} - S_{2019}}{2^{2019}}.$$

Now, we need to find S_{2019} and S_{2023}. We are given that
$$7S_n \equiv 1 \,(mod\ 2^n), \qquad n \geq 1.$$
This means that there exists an integer k such that;
$$7S_n \equiv 2^n \times k + 1$$
We can use this equation to find S_{2019} and S_{2023} as follows:
For $n = 2019$: $7S_{2019} \equiv 2^{2019} \cdot k + 1$
Taking both sides $mod\ 7$, we get: $0 \equiv 2^{2019} \cdot k + 1 \,(mod\ 7)$

Using Fermat's Little Theorem, we can simplify this as follows:
$$2^{2019} = (2^{336})^6 \times 2^3 \quad \rightarrow \quad (2^{336})^6 \equiv 1 \,(mod\ 7)$$
Therefore, we have:
$$2^{2019} \,(mod\ 7) \equiv (1) \times 2^3 \,(mod\ 7) \equiv 1 \,(mod\ 7)$$
Plugging this back into the equation $0 \equiv 2^{2019} \times k + 1 \,(mod\ 7)$, we get:
$$0 \equiv k + 1 \,(mod\ 7) \quad \rightarrow \quad k \equiv 6 \,(mod\ 7).$$
This means that:
$$7S_{2019} = 2^{2019} \cdot 6 + 1 \quad \rightarrow \quad S_{2019} = \frac{2^{2019} \cdot 6 + 1}{7}$$

For $n = 2023$: $7S_{2023} \equiv 2^{2023} \cdot j + 1$
Taking both sides $mod\ 7$, we get: $0 \equiv 2^{2023} \cdot j + 1 \,(mod\ 7)$

Using Fermat's Little Theorem, we can simplify this as follows:
$$2^{2023} = (2^{337})^6 \times 2^1 \quad \rightarrow \quad (2^{337})^6 \equiv 1 \,(mod\ 7)$$
Therefore, we have:
$$2^{2023} \,(mod\ 7) \equiv (1) \times 2 \,(mod\ 7) \equiv 2 \,(mod\ 7)$$
Plugging this back into the equation $0 \equiv 2^{2023} \times j + 1 \,(mod\ 7)$, we get:
$$0 \equiv 2j + 1 \,(mod\ 7) \quad \rightarrow \quad j \equiv 3 \,(mod\ 7).$$
This means that:
$$7S_{2023} = 2^{2023} \cdot 3 + 1 \quad \rightarrow \quad S_{2023} = \frac{2^{2023} \cdot 3 + 1}{7}$$

So,
$$\frac{S_{2023} - S_{2019}}{2^{2019}} = \frac{\dfrac{2^{2023} \cdot 3 + 1}{7} - \dfrac{2^{2019} \cdot 6 + 1}{7}}{2^{2019}}$$

Since $2^{2019} \,(mod\ 7) \equiv (1) \times 2^3 \,(mod\ 7) \equiv 1 \,(mod\ 7)$,
$$\rightarrow \quad \frac{2^{2019}(2^4 \times 3 - 6)}{7} = \frac{(1) \cdot (42)}{7} = 6.$$
Therefore, the value of the sum is 6.

84. **Answer** **(A)**

Let's start by using the given expression in terms of S_n:
$$a_{2020} + 2a_{2021} + 4a_{2022} + 8a_{2023} = \frac{S_{2024} - S_{2019}}{2^{2020}}.$$
Now, we need to find S_{2020} and S_{2024}. We are given that
$$5S_n \equiv 2 \ (mod \ 2^n), \quad n \geq 1.$$
This means that there exists an integer k such that;
$$5S_n \equiv 2^n \times k + 2$$

We can use this equation to find S_{2020} and S_{2024} as follows:
For $n = 2020$: $5S_{2020} \equiv 2^{2020} \cdot k + 2$
Taking both sides $mod \ 5$, we get: $0 \equiv 2^{2020} \cdot k + 1 \ (mod \ 5)$

Using Fermat's Little Theorem $(a^p \equiv a(mod \ p))$,
$$2^{2020} = (2^{404})^5 \quad \rightarrow \quad (2^{404})^5 \equiv 2 \ (mod \ 5)$$
Plugging this back into the equation $0 \equiv 2^{2020} \times k + 2 \ (mod 5)$, we get:
$$0 \equiv 2k + 2 \ (mod \ 5) \quad \rightarrow \quad k \equiv 4 \ (mod \ 5).$$
This means that:
$$5S_{2020} = 2^{2020} \cdot 4 + 2 \quad \rightarrow \quad S_{2020} = \frac{2^{2020} \cdot 4 + 2}{5}$$

For $n = 2024$: $5S_{2024} \equiv 2^{2024} \cdot j + 2$
Taking both sides $mod \ 5$, we get: $0 \equiv 2^{2024} \cdot j + 2 \ (mod \ 5)$

Using Fermat's Little Theorem $(a^{p-1} \equiv 1 \ (mod \ p))$,
$$2^{2024} = (2^{506})^{5-1} \quad \rightarrow \quad (2^{506})^{5-1} \equiv 1 \ (mod \ 5)$$
Therefore, we have:
$$2^{2024} \ (mod \ 5) \equiv 1 \ (mod \ 5)$$
Plugging this back into the equation $0 \equiv 2^{2024} \times j + 2 \ (mod \ 5)$, we get:
$$0 \equiv j + 2 \ (mod \ 5) \quad \rightarrow \quad j \equiv 3 \ (mod \ 5).$$
This means that:
$$5S_{2024} = 2^{2024} \cdot 3 + 2 \quad \rightarrow \quad S_{2024} = \frac{2^{2024} \cdot 3 + 2}{5}$$

So,
$$\frac{S_{2024} - S_{2020}}{2^{2020}} = \frac{\frac{2^{2024} \cdot 3 + 2}{5} - \frac{2^{2020} \cdot 4 + 2}{5}}{2^{2020}}$$
$$\rightarrow \frac{2^{2020}(2^4 \times 3 - 4)}{5 \times 2^{2020}} = \frac{44}{5} = 4.$$

Therefore, the value of the sum is 4.

Answer (**D**)

We need to find the option which is not divisible by any prime number less than 10. We can use modular arithmetic to check whether a number is divisible by a prime number or not.

(A) we can use modulo 3. If the number is divisible by 3, then it is not a correct answer. We have:
$$2^{1212} - 1 \equiv (-1)^{1212} - 1 \equiv 1 - 1 \equiv 0 \ (mod\ 3).$$
Thus, $2^{1212} - 1$ is divisible by 3.

(B) we can use modulo 5. If the number is divisible by 5, then it is not a correct answer. We have:
$$2^{606} + 1 \equiv 2^{Rem\ (606, \varphi(5))} + 1 \equiv 2^{Rem\ (606, 4)} + 1 \equiv 2^2 + 1 \equiv 0 (mod\ 5).$$
Thus, $2^{606} + 1$ is divisible by 5.
In detail, we use Fermat's Little Theorem, which states that if p is a prime number and a is an integer not divisible by p, then $a^{p-1} \equiv 1 \ (mod\ p)$. In this case, $p = 5$, so we know that $2^4 \equiv 1 \ (mod\ 5)$, because 2 is not divisible by 5.
Now, we can use the fact that if $x \equiv y(mod\ p)$, then $a^x \equiv a^y(mod\ p)$ for any integer a, to simplify the exponent of 2. We have:
$$2^{606} + 1 \equiv 2^{\left(Rem\ 606, \varphi(5)\right)} + 1 \ (mod\ 5)$$
where $\varphi(5) = 4$ is the Euler totient function of 5, which gives the number of integers less than 5 that are coprime to 5. Since $606 \equiv 2 \ (mod\ 4)$, we have:
$$2^{606} + 1 \equiv 2^{Rem\ (606, 4)} + 1 \ (mod\ 5)$$
where Rem(606, 4) is the remainder when 606 is divided by 4, which is 2. Finally, we simplify the exponent of 2 by using the fact that $2^4 \equiv 1(mod\ 5)$:
$$2^{Rem\ (606, 4)} + 1 \equiv 2^2 + 1 \ (mod\ 5)$$
because $2^2 \equiv 4 \equiv -1 \ (mod\ 5)$.
Therefore, we have shown that $2^{606} + 1$ is congruent to 0 modulo 5, which means that it is divisible by 5.

(D) we can use modulo 3. If the number is divisible by 3, then it is not a correct answer. We have:
$$2^{1213} + 1 \equiv (-1)^{1213} + 1 \equiv -1 + 1 \equiv 0 \ (mod\ 3).$$
Thus, $2^{1213} + 1$ is divisible by 3.

(E), we can use modulo 5. If the number is divisible by 5, then it is not a correct answer. We have:
$$2^{607} + 3^{607} \equiv 2^{607} + (-2)^{607} \equiv 2^{607} - 2^{607} \equiv 0 \ (mod\ 5).$$
Thus, $2^{607} + 3^{607}$ is divisible by 5.

| 86. | **Answer** | **(D)** |

We can use modular arithmetic to find the residues of $N \pmod 5$ and their corresponding remainders when raised to the 20th power.

If $N \equiv 0 \pmod 5$, then
$$N^{20} \equiv 0^{20} \equiv 0 \pmod 5$$
If $N \equiv 1 \pmod 5$, then
$$N^{20} \equiv 1^{20} \equiv 1 \pmod 5$$
If $N \equiv 2 \pmod 5$, then
$$N^{20} \equiv (N^2)^{10} \equiv (2^2)^{10} \equiv 4^{10} \equiv (-1)^{10} \equiv 1 \pmod 5$$
If $N \equiv 3 \pmod 5$, then
$$N^{20} \equiv (N^2)^{10} \equiv (3^2)^{10} \equiv 9^{10} \equiv (-1)^{10} \equiv 1 \pmod 5$$
If $N \equiv 4 \pmod 5$, then
$$N^{20} \equiv 4^{20} \equiv (-1)^{20} \equiv 1 \pmod 5$$

In four out of the five cases, the remainder when N^{20} is divided by 5 is 1. Since each case occurs equally as there are 404 residues for each residue class (mod 5) in the range $1 \le N \le 2,040$, the probability that the remainder when N^{20} is divided by 5 is 1 is $\frac{4}{5}$.

To elaborate, since each residue class occurs equally in the range, we can conclude that each of the five cases in our solution occurs with equal probability. Therefore, we can count the number of residues that have a remainder of 1 when raised to the 16th power and divide that by the total number of residues (which is 2,040) to get the probability that the remainder when N^20 is divided by 5 is 1.

| 87. | **Answer** | **(C)** |

Let the four-term arithmetic sequence be a, $a + d$, $a + 2d$, and $a + 3d$. Let the four-term geometric sequence be b, br, br^2, and br^3. Then, the resulting sequence is $a + b$, $a + d + br$, $a + 2d + br^2$, and $a + 3d + br^3$.
We are given the first three terms of the resulting sequence, which are 57, 60, and 91.
This means that:
$$a + b = 57$$
$$a + d + br = 60$$
$$a + 2d + br^2 = 91$$
We want to find the fourth term of the resulting sequence, which is $a + 3d + br^3$.

First, we can subtract the first equation from the second equation and the second equation from the third equation to get:

$$d + b(r - 1) = 3$$
$$d + br(r - 1) = 31$$

Next, we can subtract these two equations to eliminate d and get:

$$b(r - 1)^2 = 28$$

Since $(r - 1)^2$ is always a perfect square. we can note that b must be either 7 or 28. We can then proceed with casework:

If $b = 28$, then $r = 2$, $a = 29$, and $d = -25$.

The arithmetic sequence is 29,4,−21,−46, arriving at a contradiction.

If $b = 7$, then $r = 3$, $a = 50$, and $d = -11$.

The arithmetic sequence is 50, 39, 28, 17, and the geometric sequence is 7, 21, 63, 189. This case is valid.

Therefore, the value of the fourth term of the resulting four-term sequence is $a + 3d + br^3 = 17 + 189 = 206$.

---

88. *Answer* **(A)**

Let the four-term arithmetic sequence be a, $a + d$, $a + 2d$, and $a + 3d$. Let the four-term geometric sequence be b, br, br^2, and br^3. Then, the resulting sequence is $a - b$, $a + d - br$, $a + 2d - br^2$, and $a + 3d - br^3$.

We are given the first three terms of the resulting sequence, which are 59, 34, and −15.

This means that:

$$a - b = 59$$
$$a + d - br = 34$$
$$a + 2d - br^2 = -15$$

We want to find the fourth term of the resulting sequence, which is $a + 3d + br^3$.

First, we can subtract the first equation from the second equation and the second equation from the third equation to get:

$$d - b(r - 1) = -25$$
$$d - br(r - 1) = -49$$

Next, we can subtract these two equations to eliminate d and get:

$$-b(r - 1)^2 = -24 \quad \rightarrow \quad b(r - 1)^2 = 24$$

Since $(r - 1)^2$ is always a perfect square. we can note that b must be either 6 or 24. We can then proceed with casework:

If $b = 24$, then $r = 2$, $a = 83$, and $d = -1$.

The arithmetic sequence is 83, 82, 81, 80 and the geometric sequence is 24, 48, 96, 192.

So, the fourth term of this sequence is -112.
If $b = 6$, then $r = 3$, $a = 65$, and $d = -13$.
The arithmetic sequence is 65, 52, 39, 26 and the geometric sequence is 24, 48, 96, 192.
So, the fourth term of this sequence is -136.

Therefore, the fourth term of this sequence is -112 or -136.

89. **Answer** (**A**)

If the first term is a, then the sequence is;
$$a, \quad a+2, \quad a+4, \quad a+6, \quad a+8, \quad a+10, \dots .$$

Since the value of n doesn't matter in the quotient $\frac{S_{3n}}{S_n}$,
$$\frac{S_3}{S_1} = \frac{S_6}{S_2} \rightarrow \frac{3a+6}{a} = \frac{6a+30}{2a+2} \rightarrow \frac{a+2}{a} = \frac{a+5}{a+1}.$$
Using cross product;
$$a^2 + 5a = a^2 + 3a + 2 \rightarrow a = 1$$

From arithmetic sequence and series formula;
$$a_{30} = 1 + (30-1) \times 2 = 59$$
$$S_{30} = \frac{30 \times (1+59)}{2} = 900.$$

90. **Answer** (**B**)

Using the formula for arithmetic sequence's nth term,
$$a_n = a_1 + (n-1)d$$
$$79 = 15 + (n-1)4$$
So,
$$n - 1 = 16 \rightarrow n = 17$$

Therefore, there are 17 terms in the arithmetic sequence.

91. **Answer** *(A)*

The given sequence can be observed to have a pattern and find a general term for this sequence.

$a_1 = 143 = 13 \times 11 = (10^1 + 3)(10^1 + 10^0)$
$a_2 = 11433 = 103 \times 111 = (10^2 + 3)(10^2 + 10^1 + 10^0)$
$a_3 = 1114333 = 1003 \times 1111 = (10^3 + 3)(10^3 + 10^2 + 10^1 + 10^0)$
...

Thus, the nth term of the sequence can be expressed as

$$a_n = (10^n + 1) \times \sum_{k=0}^{n} 10^k$$

We can factorize each term of the sequence using this expression.

Each term can be expressed as the product of two numbers. Since every term has a factor other than 1 and itself, none of the terms of the sequence are prime.

Therefore, there are 0 prime numbers in the given sequence.

92. **Answer** *(B)*

Adding the two given equations gives: $a_1 + a_2 + \cdots + a_{200} = 600$.
Let d be the common difference. Since $a_2 - a_1 = d$, we need to find d to get the answer.

The formula for the sum of an arithmetic series is:
$$Sn = \frac{2a1 + (n-1)d}{2}$$
where n is the number of terms, a_1 is the first term, and d is the common difference.
Using this formula for the equations, we get:
$$50 \times (2a_1 + 99d) = 200 \quad \rightarrow \quad 2a_1 + 99d = 4$$
$$100 \times (2a_1 + 199d) = 600 \quad \rightarrow \quad 2a_1 + 199d = 6$$

Subtracting the first equation from the second equation, we get:
$$100d = 2, and\ d = a_2 - a_1 = \frac{2}{100} = \frac{1}{50} = 0.02.$$

93. **Answer** (D)

The sum of the given integers is $2 + 2 + 5 + 5 + 6 = 20$. Since there are 6 integers in the data set, the average (arithmetic mean) of the data set is $\dfrac{20 + D}{6}$ and the average must be greater than 3.

There are 3 possible positive integers for D.
1st if the average is 5;
$$\frac{20 + D}{6} = 5 \quad \rightarrow \quad 20 + D = 30 \quad \rightarrow \quad D = 10$$
2nd if the average is 6;
$$\frac{20 + D}{6} = 6 \quad \rightarrow \quad 20 + D = 36 \quad \rightarrow \quad D = 16$$
3rd if the average is D;
$$\frac{20 + D}{6} = D \quad \rightarrow \quad 20 + D = 6D \quad \rightarrow \quad D = 4$$

Therefore, the sum of all positive integers is $10 + 16 + 4 = 30$.

94. **Answer** (E)

The sum of the given integers is $2 + 8 + 4 + 4 + 6 + 6 = 30$. Since there are 7 integers in the data set, the average (arithmetic mean) of the data set is $\dfrac{30 + N}{7}$ and the average must be greater than 4.

There are 3 possible positive integers for N.
1st if the average is 6;
$$\frac{30 + N}{7} = 6 \quad \rightarrow \quad 30 + N = 42 \quad \rightarrow \quad N = 12$$
2nd if the average is 8;
$$\frac{30 + N}{7} = 8 \quad \rightarrow \quad 30 + N = 56 \quad \rightarrow \quad N = 26$$
3rd if the average is N;
$$\frac{30 + N}{7} = N \quad \rightarrow \quad 30 + N = 7N \quad \rightarrow \quad N = 5$$

Therefore, the sum of all positive integers is $12 + 26 + 5 = 43$.

95. *Answer* **(E)**

Let M be the median of the five positive integers, and let x and y be the two smallest integers. The two largest integers must be $M + 3$, since the unique mode is 3 greater than the median. The five integers can be sorted in increasing order as follows:

$$x, \quad y, \quad M, \quad M + 3, \quad M + 3.$$

Since the median is 3 greater than the arithmetic mean, we have

$$\frac{x + y + M + (M + 3) + (M + 3)}{5} + 3 = M$$

so,

$$x + y + 21 = 2M.$$

Note that $x + y$ must be odd, since the sum of two odd integers is even, and the sum of odd and even integers is odd.
To minimize the arithmetic mean, median, and unique mode, we can minimize the sum $x + y$.
Let $x = 1$ and $y = 2$, which gives us $M = 12$ and $M + 3 = 15$.

Therefore, the minimum possible value for the unique mode is 15.

96. *Answer* **(B)**

The mean of the five numbers is

$$\frac{3 + 5 + 7 + 12 + n}{5} = \frac{27 + n}{5}.$$

There are three possibilities for the median: it is either 5, 7, or n.

Let's consider three cases for the median:

Case 1: median and mean = 5.
In this case, n must be less than 5, since the median is the middle number in the ordered list. So we have the inequality $n < 5$. Since the mean and the median are equal,

$$\frac{27 + n}{5} = 5 \quad \rightarrow \quad n = -2$$

The sequence is -2, 3, 5, 7, 12, which does have median 5, so this is a valid solution.

Case 2: median and mean = 7.
In this case, n must be greater than 7. Since the mean and the median are equal, we have

$$\frac{27 + n}{5} = 7 \quad \rightarrow \quad n = 8.$$

The sequence is 3, 5, 7, 8, 12, which does have median 7, so this is a valid solution.

Case 3: median and mean = n.
In this case, n must be greater than 5 and less than 7. Since the mean and the median are equal, we have
$$\frac{27 + n}{5} = n \quad \rightarrow \quad 4n = 27 \quad \rightarrow \quad n = 6.75$$
However, this value of n does not satisfy the condition that n is an integer.

Therefore, the sum of integers n is $-2 + 8 = 6$.

97. Answer (B)

We are given the set $\{1, 2, 3, ..., 25\}$ and we need to choose a subset A such that the sum of any two (not necessarily distinct) elements in A is not an element of A.

First, consider the case where A contains only odd numbers. Since the sum of two odd numbers is always even, we can choose all the odd numbers from 1 to 25 and no two of them will add up to an even number. Therefore, we can include all the odd numbers from 1 to 25 in A, which gives us a total of 13 elements.

Now, let's consider the case where A contains even numbers as well. To prevent the sum of two elements in A from being an element of A, we need to make sure that no even number in A can be expressed as the sum of two even numbers or an even number and an odd number. However, since there are only 12 even numbers in the set $\{1, 2, 3, ..., 25\}$, we can only add at most 6 even numbers to A.

To add an even number to A, we must remove at least one odd number from A, because the sum of two odd numbers is always even. Therefore, for every even number we add to A, we must remove at least one odd number, which reduces the number of elements in A. So, it is not possible to have more than 13 elements in A.

Hence, the maximum number of elements in A is 13.

Answer (**D**)

To form two subsets with an intersection of exactly two elements, we first need to choose the two elements that will be present in both subsets. There are 5 choose 2 ways to do this, which gives us 10 possible pairs of elements ($_5C_2 = 10$).

Let's say we choose elements 'p' and 'q' to be in both subsets.
Now, we have to divide the remaining elements, 'r', 's', and 't', into two subsets. Each of these elements can either be in the first subset, the second subset, or neither. There are 2 choices for each of the 3 elements, so we have $2 \times 2 \times 2 = 8$ ways to divide the remaining elements into the two subsets.

However, we've counted some cases twice. For example, if we put 'r' and 's' in the first subset and 't' in the second subset, that's the same as putting 'r' and 's' in the second subset and 't' in the first subset. There are a total of 4 pairs of elements, so each case is counted twice. Therefore, we need to divide by 2 to get rid of the overcounting.

So the total number of ways to choose the two subsets is
$$\frac{10 \times 8}{2} = 40.$$

99. **Answer** (**D**)

Let **B** denote a school that is bigger than Fermat School, and **M** denote a school that sold more T-shirts than Fermat School.

The given statement "No school bigger than Fermat School sold more T-shirts than Fermat School" can be written as
$$if \ B \ then \ not \ M,$$
where **not B** denotes a school that is not bigger than Fermat School, and **not M** denotes a school that did not sell more T-shirts than Fermat School.

The contrapositive of this statement is *if M then not B*, which is equivalent to answer choice (D).

Therefore, (D) is the correct answer.

In this problem, Mr. Simon makes a promise in the form of a conditional statement: "Anyone who gets all the open-ended questions right on the upcoming exam will receive an A on the exam." This is a conditional statement, and its contrapositive is "If one does not receive an A, then he or she did not get all of the open-ended questions right."

We need to find the necessary conclusion that follows from this conditional statement. Analyzing the contrapositive, we can see that "if one does not receive an A, then he or she got at least one of the open-ended questions wrong." Rewriting this statement as a converse, we get "if one got all the open-ended questions right, then he or she received an A." This leads to the same conclusion as option (C).

However, it is simpler to negate the contrapositive and create its inverse. Negating the contrapositive gives us "If one does not get all of the open-ended questions right, then he or she does not receive an A." Rewriting this statement as an inverse, we get "If one got at least one of the open-ended questions wrong, then he or she did not receive an A." This leads to the same conclusion as option (B).

Therefore, the answer is (B). Option (B) is the negation of the contrapositive of the conditional statement. (That is, it has been negated as well as reversed.)

Made in the USA
Las Vegas, NV
04 October 2024

96321115R00052